# BECOMING DEBRA WRIGHT

DEBRA WRIGHT

# Becoming Debra Wright

*~A Memoir Of Overcoming Overwhelming Obstacles Yet Still Standing **Strong**~*

Debra Wright

Copyright © 2019 by Debra Wright

All rights reserved. This book or any portion thereof may not be reproduced or used in any manner whatsoever without the express written permission of the publisher except for the use of brief quotations in a book review.

Printed in Canada First Printing, 2019

Melodicrose Publishing

www.melodicrosepublishing.com

***This book is dedicated to my parents Percy and Maria Caprietta.***

*Your life has been a testament of faith and commitment to each other, your children and your God. I remember when life was tough but you made sure we all were ok. For your unconditional love and taking the time to show me what true love is;*
*Thank you.*

*For believing in me and being one of the strong supporters*
*I could always count on;*
*Thank you*

*I love you Mom and Dad!*

## ACKNOWLEDGMENTS

**To my husband and best friend Carlton:** Thank you for your support and encouragement to be all that I could be and for not being afraid to let me shine. It means the world to me. *I love you.*

**My Children:** Christie-Ann, Joseph and Christopher, thank you for being my rock during those difficult days and I know that each one of you will continue to grow and excel in everything that you do. *I love you to the moon and beyond.*

**Maurice, Jenecia and Bethany** my bonus blessings, I have accepted and love you with all my heart. As we continue on this journey, you will continue to excel in all you do. Thank you for being a part of my life.

**To my siblings and their spouses:** You know who you are, for all the love, support and the encouragement to follow my dream. Thank you.

**To Cindy:** My daughter, sister and friend, for always being there. Love you.

**To my mentor Marcia Y. Ford:** Thank you for guiding me through the process of writing this book. Much love.

**To my Editors and Publisher at Melodicrose Publishing:** Thank you for your feedback and great direction in bringing this book to the market.

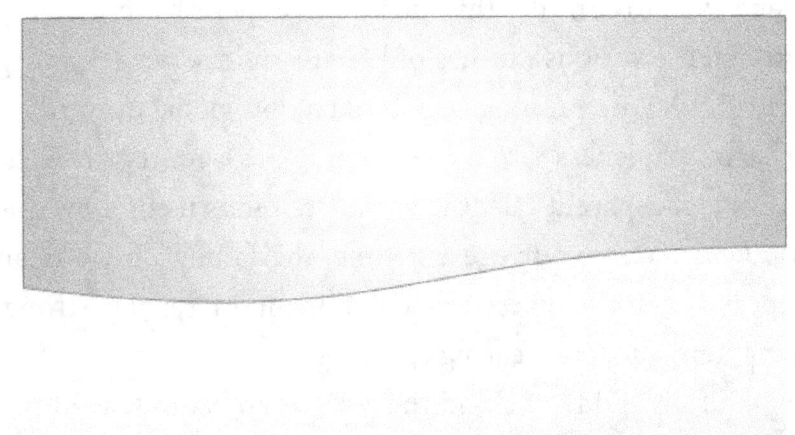

# Forward

## FOREWORD

If one were to consider this memoir as a thesis for navigating through the various hurdles of life, it would serve as a much needed tool in pushing the broken individual towards a sense of wholeness. From the opening passages of this well-weaved transparent tale, the author reminds us of a bygone era, when unlike our present time, the family unit was an important, if not necessary component in raising strong, competent and God-fearing children.

Skillfully hidden behind the story that Debra tells of her upbringing, of her time of mistreatment at the hands of her teachers, the strictness of her parents, the enjoyment of having a large close-knit family, her rebellion, her losses, her sickness, her regrets and ultimate triumph, is the fact that hers was a life that was built on a firm foundation, that foundation being Jesus Christ.

Her parents trained up their children in the way that they should go, with the presence of mind that when they grew old, they will not depart from it. (Proverbs 22:6).

In her writing Debra states "Prayer and a strong faith in God were the glue that kept us in those day."

The transparency of mistakes, that some will call youthful indiscretions, is key to healing and it will serve to encourage the readers that there is a necessary process that one must go through before they are able to walk in God's healing.

Her advice on marriage, infidelity and divorce, on what it takes to have a successful marriage, and what is necessary to survive it, is inspirational and tutorial.

FOREWORD

Through every hard journey, coming to the place where one can say, "Today I can see how far I have come," should be the goal of everyone who is currently in their journey.

Finally, there is a clarion call in the pages of this book for the "Deborah" of this generation…."**Awake, awake**, Deborah: **awake, awake**, utter a song: arise," (Judges 5:12).

-**Apostle Glen Prince**, Senior Leader, Ruach Ministries, Elgin, I. Author of *The Birth of A Vision*

# Preface

## PREFACE

I am terrified of baring my soul. Writing my memoir was something I struggled with, because it scared me that I would be letting people into my sacred space. However, I felt a pressing upon my spirit that I should begin the process to share my experiences in the hope that it would help someone along their journey. As the Chinese proverb says, "**A journey of a thousand miles begins with a single step.**"

I am the first born of seven children and obviously, that's a lot of pressure. I have two sisters and, four brothers. Each one, successful in their own right. Growing up in the Caprietta household was very interesting to say the least; our family was very close-knit and very loving. Our parents, Percy and Maria were strict God-fearing people and instilled in us a deep and strict moral code. I remember many mornings our father would wake us up to pray and have bible studies. Sometimes, it was so hard to stay awake. We would pull the sheets over our heads and hope our parents wouldn't notice, this gave us a few extra minutes of sleep. As kids, we did not like getting up so early. However studying God's word as a family, gave my siblings and I the foundation we needed that has helped throughout our entire lives. My father wanted to know that his children had a relationship with the God that he served. I loved going to church even if I did not understand some of the doctrines that was preached. We learned to honor God and to serve him to the best of our abilities.

Growing up in such an atmosphere where the spiritual side of things was uppermost in our daily thoughts and actions, it became relatively easy to take on the challenges of life, or its frills, in our strides with ease of heart as children and as adults.

When the ride became rough in the course of life, we made it a habit to always remember the moral foundations of our growth process, which were the very tenets of my father's convictions. When everything else seemed smooth, we did not forget that it was the grace of our Maker at play. These aspects invariably helped to balance the scale of life for me and my siblings.

This memoir, therefore, is simply my effort to perceive of life firstly as a journey. A mixture of both the sublime and challenging experiences, could overwhelm the individual, if they are not properly grounded in the spirit.

Secondly, the experience of life has also taught me that this tortuous journey is often a learning curve. The combination of the 'good, the bad and the ugly' sums up the experiences of all mortals, and make us either better individuals who turn the tides of life for good, or become consumed by their sheer force. This, I believe, is the essence of this memoir; to inspire us all to move away from the edge of despair and self-pity, to the realm of liberty of the mind and spirit. So be willing to embrace positive change when it knocks on your doors, and be willing to make the most of it when it matters, for therein lies man's true liberation.

~Chapter One~

# The Early Years

I was born in a small village in Trinidad, called Febeau Village, Laventille Road to be exact. This village is located in the small town of San Juan. It is nestled between the San Juan – Laventille Region and the East-West Corridor Metropolitan area between Barataria and Saint Joseph. Febeau Village was a very interesting place. Many people lived on the hills but some of us lived in the valley. If I could paint the picture it would be; the road was on the top and our house was in the valley below. We had lots of fruit trees in our yard, coconuts, cherries, mangoes, avocados and some citrus trees, as well. Our neighborhood had a very eclectic mix of people, we had grandmothers and aunts galore. It was just our culture. We were raised to be respectful to our elders and for the most part, this worked well for us. It was just as the saying goes, "It takes a village to raise a child." Our neighbors looked out for the village kids.

At the back of our property was a ravine, which separated us from our neighbors on the hillside.

My mom grew up in Laventille Road, with her parents and siblings. Grandpa was a minister of the gospel and a very powerful preacher. He was fearless and would preach wherever he went, sometimes in front of the rum shop, on the street corner. Everyone knew Reverend Harold Jackman and his family well. He even had a church built on the property and many people would come to hear the word of God.

My grandparents had twelve children. As a postman and a preacher, my grandpa was able to reach a lot of people on his journey, good and bad. I remember hearing a story about how fearless Grandpa was and how he truly trusted his God. The story was told that coming home late one night, a group of young men in the village, who were really upset with my grandfather because of his stance on their behavior of drinking and living promiscuous lives, decided to beat him up that night. As they were waiting on him, it was told that Reverend Jackman had an army walking with him and they all ran away. It was not a physical army but just as the prophet Elijah's servant was afraid of the army surrounding them back then, God allowed those young men to see the host of his army surrounding my grandfather. It was God protecting him that night and he became a man to be feared.

He planted churches in Trinidad and Tobago and migrated to Canada, after his wife passed away. He continued to work in the ministry and was a light to the Regent Park community in Toronto, Canada and beyond. The loss of his wife caused him and their children a lot of pain. My mother helped to care for some of her younger siblings. She was pregnant with me when her mother passed away and she had a hard time coping with my impending birth so soon after the death.

My mother told me that she had me at home because she was afraid to go to the hospital. You see, my grandmother passed away just a few months before I was born, during the birth of her last baby. This was a very traumatic experience for my mother. While attending the maternity clinic, Mom had a lot of anxiety. She told the nurses that she was afraid that she would die if she had to go to the hospital for my birth, just like her mother before her. She was given the option to deliver at home or at the hospital but if there were any complications she would have to go to the hospital. She agreed and promptly decided to give birth to me, at home.

Mom went through Christmas and New Year's Day, pregnant with me. Her labor started on the night of January 1st. On January 2nd, 1967, I was born. It was a joyous time in the family, at my birth. Our family was excited as I was the first of the grandchildren that had been born. I could only imagine the atmosphere; a new life comes into the world after having lost two lives, months earlier.

The year 1967 was a very interesting year for our country; it became the first Commonwealth country to join the Organization of American States (OAS).

According to wikipedia, "The Republic of Trinidad and Tobago are twin islands located in the southernmost part of the Caribbean. It was discovered by Christopher Columbus in 1498 and was colonized by the Spanish until the Spanish Governor Jose Maria Chacon surrendered to the British in 1797. Trinidad and Tobago gained its independence from the United Kingdom on 31 August 1962, and a Republic in in the Commonwealth in 1976".

It is often said that the time we are born has a lot to do with our personalities, and I've found that to be very true. A person born in January is known to be very ambitious, exhibit leadership traits, loves people and is gifted as well as focused on business. This describes me, as I see these qualities very evident by the things that I gravitate to and how

I interact with those around me. My sister and daughter are also born in the month of January. Mom, though not born in January, carries the same astrological sign. These qualities are very evident in them, as well.

Mom worked as a food service supervisor in the hospital and Dad was a barber by trade and he did that until he retired. My dad worked at a barbershop in the San Juan market, or as they called it, the "Croisee". When I became a teenager, I would take lunch to my father. I loved going to the market. After delivering his lunch, I would go to the market and get produce to take home for my mother. While shopping, I would always make sure to purchase a sandwich of hops bread (similar to a dinner roll) and ham with a glass of mauby (made from the bark of the mauby tree.) Aww! That was so good.

After a few years of life being great, the economy started to slow down and times were hard for many families including ours. I remember my dad's eldest brother worked at a company called Sunshine Snacks in Trinidad and he would come by our home with big bags of snacks and food stuff in bulk, to help us make it through the rough times. My parents were not too proud to accept the help. When our cousins needed snacks or food we would always share what we had with them.

My parents loved each other so much. Even during those hard times, they held it together and our family became even stronger. Prayer and a strong faith in God was the glue that kept us in those times.

After that tough spell during the late 1970's, life was pretty good for the most part; we had lots of fun and did most things together, as a family. In the early 1980's, Dad got a job in the Trinidad and Tobago Defense Force, as the barber. He was also the personal barber to Sir Ellis Clarke, who was the second and last Governor-General of Trinidad and Tobago and the first President of Trinidad and Tobago. He was one of the main architects of Trinidad and Tobago's 1962 Independence constitution. I guess you can say, my father was famous in his own rights.

While my father was employed in the army, he would take us to a place called Chaguaramas, close to the army base where he worked. There was a beach there, called Carenage and we would spend the day bathing and fishing. Sometimes, Dad would take our cousins along with us and boy it was a lot of fun. I guess this is why I love the ocean so much. I could spend all day at the beach and be so at peace. It was during this time, my paternal grandmother, Mama as she was called, came to live with us for a while. My father's sister Mary and her daughter Jules lived with us, as well. Even though it was a full house, there was lots of love. Our house had three bedrooms but we were able to fit eleven persons in there.

In the early 70's, my siblings and I attended the San Juan Presbyterian Primary School, which was located on one of the main streets leading to our little village. During my time at this school, I had some tough experiences that coloured my world for a long time. Our school population was predominantly of East Indian descent. My siblings and I were mistreated by some of our teachers. I am not really sure why we had such a rough time but I remember getting beaten by a wooden ruler or a leather belt for minor reasons. Many students were abused by the teachers in this way. Our hands would be red and sometimes blistered. I remember one time not being able to spell a word correctly and my teacher gave me three lashes in my hand. This was very painful. Corporal punishment was still in effect in Trinidad and Tobago, and across the Caribbean. It was used for disciplining the children at home and school and became a form of abuse in many cases. I was so angry! One of my younger brothers had a much harder time and I wished our parents would move us out of the school. We all stayed and completed our common entrance exams to go into high school, and finally left that environment.

Corporal punishment was finally banned in schools in Trinidad and Tobago in 2001.

Most days, we walked about 3.5 kilometers from our home to school and also returned home the same way. Sometimes, the distance was a bit too much because the sun was really hot or, at times, it was raining, but we got used to it and continued our education. There were times when my parents would hire a taxi to pick us up from school and when Dad purchased our first car, he would pick us up from school on the days he finished work early.

Many times, I was bullied before and after school. We were different from most of our school mates because of our religion. As girls, we wore our school skirts much longer than that of our peers and we never wore pants. To some of the students, we were considered weird and they would pick on us. I was not really a fighter back then, but my mouth was considered very saucy. On many occasions, I was teased because I had full lips and was called a lot of really awful names because of it. I hated my lips and would think of how I could make it smaller. This continued into my teenage years.

One day, my sister and I were walking along the Eastern Main road on our way home from school. Our Grandfather, who we called "Papa", was a fisherman by trade. He was on his way home after a fishing trip. He saw us and stopped to pick us up. Instead of taking us home to our parents, he took us to his home in a village called La Canoa. We were having fun with our aunts and did not even think that our parents would be worried. We had no telephone, at that time, therefore, could not contact them. They were very upset and when we got home, we got a good spanking. Papa apologized; he just saw his grandchildren and did not think about us getting home late. Trust me, we never did that again. Sadly my grandfather passed away when I was thirteen years old. The funeral was very traumatic for us kids. Our grandfather was a very prolific man and had many children. It was during his funeral that we we met all our aunts and uncles for the first time, some who were even younger than us. We were all together crying and hugging each other.

My paternal grandfather also had many children and a few years ago, I had the opportunity to meet all my aunts and uncles on my father's side again after thirty years. We have grown very close and have great love and respect for one another.

Some memories that still stand out to this day; Dad would take us kids in this little car he had, a white Dodge Avenger, and we'd fit all seven kids and our mom in it. He would take us to Dairy Queen for ice cream after prayer meeting on a Friday night or to a fried chicken restaurant called Chuck Wagon. Our parents raised us to love God and serve others. They sacrificed a lot to make sure that we had what we needed and then what we wanted. There was a definite balance. Mom taught us to take care of the home and how to serve a husband. This was very big for my mother; she took care of Dad and he took care of her. Even to this day, after being married for over fifty years, my parents still treat each other with love and respect. I have always admired my mom but I was also afraid of her. Mom was used by God as a prophetess and so if we did anything bad during the day or a few days before our family prayer time, we would be so afraid to come in front of our mom. She always knew!

There is a very vivid memory as a child about my mother in a very prophetic moment. We went to a church in a small village and the pastor, his wife and some of the members were engaging in unthinkable behavior. The morning we went to church, I can remember so clearly, the place felt gloomy like the sun was hiding behind the clouds, afraid to come out. Mom stood up and began to speak to us in an unknown language, but the people that were carrying on unbecomingly heard her in English. We could hear people screaming, crying and running out of the church building. Our home was filled with so many people coming to our home to speak with Mom and as a child I could not understand. It wasn't until I was older, that I realized what had happened. God used her to take care of a wrong situation in the church. I could tell you story after story of how God used this amazing woman of God, but that's her story to tell.

We were a family with strong Christian values and church was our life. We left that church and found another church to fellowship after this incident. Years later, my dad became a pastor and we had our church in the backyard of our home, the same church that my grandfather had built and served in, years before. We lived in the church. We were the preacher's kids and they would say today PK's.

Entrepreneurship was always a part of my life. My grandmother taught me how to make sugar cake, made from grated coconut, spices and sugar. It is cooked on the stove and then put on banana leaves to cool and form a nice crusted cake. I would make, package, and then sell them at school or in my neighborhood. I made good money for a ten-year-old. I did not stop there, I started crocheting and crocheted pillows and decorative dolls, during the Christmas season. I sold the pillows for fifty dollars a pair and a doll was seventy-five each.

That was good money for a teenager and I was really efficient at fulfilling all of the orders I had. I also started teaching people how to crochet and eventually the people I taught could now make their own. I then picked up the art of macramé and also made money making and selling my crafts. People would always call me to do something or the other because I was really good at what I did and prided myself on perfecting my craft. My parents were proud of me during those times. The neighborhood kids loved coming to our home and I had a little school under our house, where I taught them how to bake cakes and some little delicacies. I was barely twelve years old.

Our Famous Car that held 9 people

Dad meeting Sir Ellis Clark, The former President of Trinidad and Tobago

The Caprietta Children

The Caprietta Family

Me on our street, Laventille Road

The view of the street in front of our house

*Chapter 2*

# The Teenage Years

*⁷ Do not remember the sins of my youth and my rebellious ways; according to your love remember me, for you, LORD, are good.*

**-Psalm 25:7 New International Version (NIV)**

In my teenage years, I became a little rebellious, chafing at the house rules and trying to forge my own identity. This caused my parents a lot of grief and pain. I just wanted to be a normal teenager with less rules and regulations. Church had its own set of rules and coupled with the rules at home, it felt very stifling. Our church was very rigid about what we could and could not do. We went to church twice on Sunday, Wednesday and Friday, so a lot of time was spent in church.

Sometimes, it was great because we had a sense of community. We could spend time with some of the young people our age and we also got in trouble with our parents. The young people at the church we went to, all had issues with the rules and laws of the church. Sometimes, I felt that I would be blamed for all the crazy stuff that they got into. Being a teenager, I often wanted to go out with my classmates and peers who were not from the church community, and I wanted to come home a little later than the curfew was. Truth be told, I didn't even remember or know what my curfew was. It was mostly no. If we were going to church or going out with the family, that would be okay.

I was in high school at Barataria Senior Comprehensive

and completed my last two years of school. I took Food and Nutrition as my major and did really well except in math. which was a subject that eluded me. I graduated from high school at the age of sixteen and got an award in food and nutrition and English.

I was seventeen when I became a student at John Donaldson Technical Institute as part of the Catering and Cafeteria Management Program. I really enjoyed cooking and setting the table for our family dinners. I was also planning meals for my church friends and family. I guess I developed my love for cooking from watching my mom. Seeing her teaching and working in the field made me want to be just like her when I grew up.

During my time there, I was a part of the Youth for Christ Association and enjoyed it, tremendously. I made some really wonderful friends, who I am still friends with to this day. During my last year in school, we organized a concert and a retreat. We had pink and grey uniforms made for the choir. I can still remember how well it went and how proud our families were of us. That weekend, we had planned a retreat and I wanted to attend. I begged and pleaded with my parents but they would not let me go. That hurt so much. We were all young Christian people with a mission to save the world and I was not allowed to be there. I was almost eighteen, well seventeen and a half, to be exact. This incident caused a lot of frustrated and I couldn't understand why I had to miss this amazing trip.

When my friends came back, they were talking about

their experience at camp. I had to sit there and listen to all that they did, with such envy. I was so upset with my parents. I did not want to speak with them at all, but that did not last very long.

I wanted to study nursing, so I had to retake a math class at night school, in order to get my math grade higher as it was not one of my better subjects at school. I came home on this one particular night a little later than normal. My father felt that I should have been home earlier, even though I tried to explain to him that there were no taxis on the stand and I had to wait a bit longer to get one. If this happened during the day, I would be able to walk the three and a half kilometers home, but it was after eight in the night. This would not have been a good option as the crime rate had started to climb. While I was waiting, I met a girlfriend who was also waiting for a taxi to go into our village and that helped me not to worry too much about how late it was getting. We kept each other company and we were able to get a taxi together and that put my mind at ease.

Coming home late caused a huge argument between my dad and I. We really had it out that night. Dad was very upset with me. I remember it clearly, the sofa was brown with checkered cushions, the lights were on bright and my siblings were in the bedroom. This was the night I told my father I did not love him. This of course, was not true, but I was so upset that he would not listen to my explanation and felt that he was not trying to see my point of view. I regretted saying that to my father because it really hurt him.

I guess being the eldest child, I was held to a higher standard so that I could be an example to the younger ones. The next day, I woke up feeling really ill and my body started swelling, my knees and ankles were affected mostly. This swelling happened throughout my childhood where, my knees would swell and walking would be painful. On two occasions fluid had to be drained and the doctors thought I had rheumatic fever or another autoimmune disease. *Thankfully this was not the case!*

That day, I ended up in the hospital, my knees and ankles swollen, in pain and very scared. Mom took me and we had to wait for a while, but finally, a really cute doctor came in to see me with another doctor. Doctor Orin, whom, I later learned was a Resident, or as we said back then, an Intern. I never knew who the other guy was. I only had eyes for Dr. Orin. This young man stood out to me and after having to go to the hospital clinic for several months, I got to know him very well. He was charming and really caring but was also guarded at times. We did not get together until a year later, when I was no longer a patient.

This relationship caused me to act in ways that was not becoming of a Christian young woman. It was love at first sight for me. We had an instant connection and my emotions were out of control. We became intimate and after that very first time, I became pregnant. I did not carry my pregnancy to full-term. This was the worst decision of my life. I wish I was stronger and said no to the termination of my pregnancy. I was afraid of hurting my parents as my dad was a minister and we practically lived in church. The church was in our backyard. I have lived with that regret for a very long time. I have, however, forgiven myself and Orin also. Many people might say, "why did you choose to do such a thing?" The answer for me would be because of fear and pressure. I was a young woman dating an older, more experienced man who did not want a baby at this time.

Life changed for me, then! This experience caused my parents so much heartache. They felt that because Orin was seventeen years older than me, he should have protected me. There were things about him that my parents were not comfortable with. I became a little withdrawn and I dreamt of that baby so many nights. I cried a lot during those days and wished I could turn back the clock. I could have lost my life that day and ended up in the hospital for almost a week. One day, my family and I were driving through the countryside and whilst driving, it seemed that a young girl was walking along the countryside and she said to me "Mom don't worry I am okay." I just cried more but I did it, silently. Until this day, I don't know if I fell asleep or what happened.

Mom cried and I could hardly look at her because of the hurt I saw in her eyes. She also had to deal with my situation alone as Dad had travelled to the United States. One of the young men took me to the hospital and many years later became my husband.

I don't think people understood the pressure of being the child of a pastor. All eyes were on my family. I was supposed to be an example to the young people in our church and also to my younger siblings. I failed miserably!

So what does a parent do during times like this? They shipped me off to my grandparents in Toronto, Canada.

I did not mind travelling to Canada. In fact, I was happy to do so. However, I missed my love immensely. We kept in touch. I started college and quickly adapted to the Canadian way of life. This was eye-opening. The sights and culture gave me a sense of wholeness and slowly my life became normal. Even though, I still missed him, terribly, I began to grow and experience life without a lot of the rules from my parents' home and soon there was no rebellion left in me. I went to the theatre with my aunts to see the play Showgirls, it was awesome! I also visited many sites around Toronto, the Canadian National Exhibition and Niagara Falls to name a few.

There were many times I wanted to go back home but I stayed and finished my schooling. I had a purpose for being in Canada and made sure I studied hard and got good grades.

My aunts were really supportive of me during my time at my grandparents' home. They made sure I had everything I needed and lacked nothing. I always remember them and have remained close to them, even to this day. Sadly, one of my aunts passed away.

One day, a friend of my parents told my mother that Orin was previously married and not divorced. Mom called me and I called him. We had a heated conversation and that was it! At that time, I wished he had been honest with me. I don't think that it would have been a problem for me. If you love someone you will try to understand their situation. He became angry, because he wanted to tell me, himself. It was fifteen years before we spoke again. One must understand the culture of a small island, everyone is in your life and knows how to find out information about you, that you thought was hidden.

I was sad. I could not understand how the relationship could end so suddenly. I moved on but there is something to say about soul ties. I had not really closed that chapter of my life and years later it would surface with serious consequences.

Over the course of twenty-five years, whenever things didn't go well in my life, my mind would wander off and the past would come back as though it was yesterday.

At the age of twenty, I graduated from the Career Canada College as a Medical Laboratory Assistant. I had to do a job placement and I was hired before my placement was finished. I stayed in this field for almost thirty years. While I was in college, a young man whom I knew from Trinidad decided to visit me for my graduation. I was excited to see him because we had become friends during the last few years before I left Trinidad. It was funny, although we were born in different years, our birthdays were one day apart. This was always an inside joke for us and I guess it gave us a bond as friends. He was introduced to us through the church my father pastored and they also worked together. We had great times as young people at church. On the nights when we had church, these young people would come straight from work and I would prepare dinner for everyone. I had no idea the young men was looking on so that they could find a wife.

One thing I could say about our little church back then was that we knew how to pray and worship God. We loved each other like we were related by blood. We would go to extraordinary lengths to help each other. We truly exemplified the love of christ. Just as in the bible, the disciples stood by one another, after Jesus was gone. We ate together, the young women shared a bed and sometimes even the shower when we were late for church. It was innocent and beautiful. On a Sunday afternoon we visited sick people in the hospital and prayed for them. Those were the good ole days.

We went out with a group of our friends, to visit the Grand Revere River. The river was located in a little town called Toco, which is the most northeasterly village on the island of Trinidad in the County of Saint David at the point where the Caribbean Sea and the Atlantic Ocean meet. Tobago lies only some thirty-five kilometers to the northeast which renders Toco the closest point in Trinidad to the sister island. We built a fire on the bank of the river and cooked a pot of pelau, ( a local one pot dish made with meat, peas, carrots, coconut milk and rice).

We swam, we ate and had the most amazing time at the river. The water was cold but refreshing; it was shaded by trees that formed an alcove above it with streams of sunlight streaming through it. Life back then was simple. This particular trip was very memorable because it was my last time there before I left for Canada two days later. After leaving Toco, we drove to my friends' home and instead of going directly to the house, we went to the Tacarigua conservation area. We walked through the forested area, seeing all the really tall bamboo plants and lots of plants native to Trinidad and Tobago. We talked about life and my leaving to study. I had no idea John was looking at me as anyone other than a sister in Christ and a friend. A few years later John said he was trying to tell me how he felt then about me but he never did till much later.

My grandmother was very intuitive and told me later during his stay in Toronto, that John came to ask for me to marry him or go out with him. I laughed so hard but she was so right. I told her he was too short and Mum, as we all called her, being very wise just laughed and told me, "We will see." That summer, we grew close and enjoyed each other's company. We visited Edwards Gardens for our first date chaperoned by one of my aunts and dined at Pizza Hut. Those were uncomplicated days and we really enjoyed it.

During the summer, my family planned a picnic, where all the kids and adults just enjoyed themselves. My father had come to Toronto. John and my dad got along really well. It was my father that led him to Christ. You can say, he was a spiritual father to him. Daddy approved of us being in a relationship. When we called our families back in Trinidad to tell them that we were together, they were all stunned. I remember John's mother mentioning that he had a communication problem. Courageously I told her not to worry, I would get him to talk to me.. How wrong I was.

John came back to Toronto for that Christmas season and brought a ring with him. We were engaged on Christmas Eve 1987. We enjoyed the holidays, and did some sightseeing to Niagara Falls and the CN Tower. My family came together for Christmas and it was such an incredible time. We celebrated our birthdays and he left for Trinidad right after that.

My Sister and I

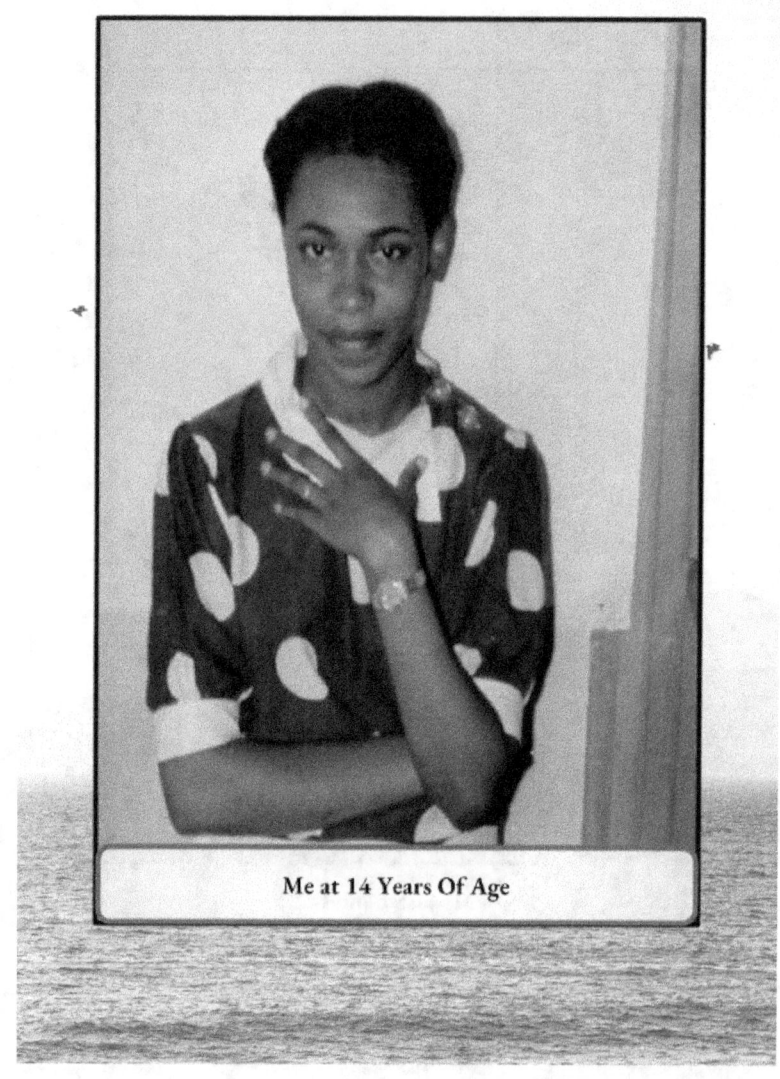

Me at 14 Years Of Age

High School with my English teacher (1981)

Me ( This photo was taken in front of our church in 1985)

Leaving Trinidad in 1986

Graduation from Career Canada College 1987

My Grandparents Harold and Iris Jackman

~Chapter Three~

# My Marriage

John and I courted long distance for the next seven months. We were married in Trinidad in nineteen eighty-eight. I really did not enjoy our wedding day, the ministers who performed the ceremony were really mechanical and very stuffy. They preached a long sermon and when the vows were done, the minister never said you may kiss the bride. Who does that? That's the highlight of the wedding after the vows. We took our photos at the University of the West Indies and then went to the reception. Our wedding was huge, we had over four hundred guests. The community centre where it was held was small and so crowded. This was actually a caribbean wedding where people invite themselves. I don't remember ever cutting our cake or anything like that. I did have a good time but a lot of it was a blur. My aunts came down with me and as well as another girlfriend, from my grandfather's church.

Life, for the first three months was magical. I went back to Trinidad and enjoyed the warmth of the Caribbean, we were in love and did a lot together, while I was there, but I longed to come back home to Toronto. We were married in April and by June I was ready to leave again. I left for Toronto. During those months I was excited for my husband to come home. I rented an apartment, got it all prepared and anxiously waited for him. My husband came to Canada a few months later. When we were finally reunited I knew something had changed. I could not put a finger on what it was, but there was a distance that we could not bridge. This left me feeling confused and searching for answers. When I left we were in a good place.

In hindsight it's difficult to determine why the disconnect happened. I believe that my leaving so quickly put us out of sync. We spoke everyday and I did not pick up on anything not being alright, Perhaps, it's because I left so soon after the marriage or maybe we both changed? This had an adverse effect on our marriage. Regardless of the reason, there was an enormous rift that began to surface in our relationship. On the very first night that my husband arrived from Trinidad, I had a strange dream. I dreamt that I went to prison. I was crying and telling the judge that I did not do anything, why was I going to prison? In all honesty, my life felt like a prison.

There were times that my mother would call from Trinidad and that would be a problem for John. I grew up really close to her and we were used to speaking on a daily basis. In my eyes, this did not diminish my relationship with John, but it became a bone of contention throughout the marriage. We had many arguments about it and throughout our entire marriage, my family was always an issue that we could never work through.

During the time that my husband left for Trinidad, there was a mass exodus of people leaving the country, and my family was also a part of this exodus.

My father and two younger brothers stayed with us, along with three other families in a very small house. The tension caused many issues for us and my husband and I grew more distant. The lack of privacy, coupled with the fact that people were stepping over each other, became a boiling point. I felt the weight of it all on my shoulder.

One can only imagine the profound chaos that we lived in. The bathroom was mildewed. We were also struggling financially. Liver became the main protein staple at most of our meals. We found a plethora of ways to cook it. I hate liver now, but back then it was what we could afford. The challenges of managing our finances and the constant stress caused us to grow further apart. We were struggling financially and all this tension caused us to grow further apart. At the age of Twenty-Two, My husband stopped communicating with me, it was heart wrenching. I was accustomed to being the life of my family home, always planning parties and fun things to do.

I felt so alone even though the house was full; so you can understand how difficult it would be to just be so quiet all the time. It was during those times, I realized I was expecting our first child. Pregnancy did not agree with my body and I spent a lot of time in hospital with a condition known as hyperemesis. I was dehydrated and could hardly stand. Years later, a friend of mine, a physician told me it could have been a direct correlation with the amount of stress I was under.

It was so hard, spending so much time in hospital alone. I spent a lot of time crying and I would read love stories to escape the pain or watch all the soap operas on television.

The hospital was my second home. I started feeling better and I was finally released and started working again.

One day I went to work and as I was about to board the train, a young woman punched me in the stomach. Why? I don't know.

I ended up at Mt. Sinai Hospital in Toronto. The pain and bleeding started when I arrived at the hospital and continued to get worse from there. I spent the night at Mt. Sinai Hospital and then was transported to the Scarborough General Hospital where I struggled to hold on to my pregnancy. I had excruciating pain for three days and on June 4th, 1989, our daughter Hannah was born prematurely. I was twenty one weeks pregnant. It was very traumatic, holding this little life that would not live even for one hour. I was devastated! I held her in my arms, wrapped in a little blanket and my heart was just breaking for my daughter that I would never bring home. I looked at her face, so beautiful and so tiny. All her ten fingers and ten toes; perfect in every way. Her father and I just sat on the bed and the tears were streaming down our faces. I am writing this now and I can still see the delivery room, the smells, the lights and then the deafening silence. My parents came to the hospital that Sunday afternoon and we all shed some tears. My grandmother came to visit, as well. She held me as I cried and told me everything would be fine.

Unless you have gone through the loss of a child, you cannot really imagine the pain one feels. There is an intense pain and you wonder when it will pass. There is a hole where your heart is supposed to be. I felt like someone had cut me in tiny pieces and I didn't want to live or see the sunshine because my life felt like a dark cloud that wouldn't lift. I was discharged from the hospital, we went to stay at my grandparents home and one day later began to experience labor pains again. We went to the hospital only to discover that there was fetal tissue from another baby. They believed it was a host twin that was not delivered previously. Thankfully, God brought us through that ordeal.

Two months later, I was pregnant with our second child who we refer to always as Jr. and at eighteen week, I felt a sharp cramp in my stomach and lots of blood started coming down my legs. I was so afraid and I cried out, "Lord, please! Not again."

Upon our arrival at the hospital, we went through the process and the doctor and nurses said it was the neatest thing to see the baby still in the sac moving around when they were doing the examination. My nurse friend, Stephanie, was a real great help to me during that period, and to this day, we have remained great friends.

With this episode, the doctors were able to diagnose my condition as an incompetent cervix and tried to help me. I got a procedure called a Shirodkar suture done to help my son stay in the womb; but in a couple hours after the procedure my water broke. The doctors kept me in the hospital, monitoring my condition and the baby. From what they told me, the water stopped leaking and my baby was Ok. I spent Christmas day and my twenty-third birthday in hospital and was discharged on January 3rd. The next night, I was burning up with fever and in the worst pain of my life. I began bleeding and was shivering with cold. My husband called 911 and on January 5th, 1990, we lost our son, as well. With this one, however, my life was very much in danger. My body became septic and I almost died. My father came to the hospital room and he began to pray together with my mom because he sensed the spirit of death present in the room. At some point, I couldn't even remember where I was and was told by my mother that I had tubes everywhere.

I was hemorrhaging and the doctors could not stop it for a long while. My doctor had to take great measure to get the bleeding stopped.

The Lord heard the cry of my parents! I stayed in hospital for about a week after delivery and was told not to become pregnant for about six months. I was discharged and we went home a week later.

Three months later, we were pregnant again! Lord, how do I tell my family? My parents were scared, my grandparents and my siblings were worried. I was worried too, but we wanted a baby so badly. This time I wasn't really trying but we did not do anything to prevent pregnancy. Sometimes we don't consider the other person's well-being and things happen.

So we got the test done which confirmed I was carrying another life. We kept silent for two months until the vomiting started and I had to go in to the hospital again. The reality? Our marriage was in trouble and because I was stressed out, my body was reacting badly to being pregnant.

Stress can do many strange things to your body. This book is in no way intended to cause hurt to my ex-husband, we are actually on good terms now. This is my experience!

At ten weeks, my doctor suggested that we would have to put a suture in at the twelfth week to keep my baby in, but just at that point, I began to bleed heavily. Upon completing an ultrasound, it was diagnosed that my placenta was torn and I needed to rest. The doctor wanted to see if that would help.

Friends, this is where I really learned to trust God. The bible says in *Proverbs 3:5 and 6 Trust in the LORD with all thine heart; and lean not unto thine own understanding. In all thy ways acknowledge him, and he shall direct thy paths. (KJV)*

A dear friend of mine, Sheree, who was also pregnant at the time, took me for a second opinion. The first doctor told me to abort my baby since the bleeding was heavy and it was just ten weeks gestation. This statement made my friend so angry that she decided to take me to her family doctor. This doctor, an elderly gentleman, sat me down and he said to me, "Young lady, children are a gift from God, so just put it in His hands."

Wow, I thought to myself. I am going to do just that. This was a Tuesday and we had church later that evening. During the service I was so scared, and I went outside to the restroom. My girlfriend, Sheree followed me in and we just began to pray.

I said, "Lord, I can't lose this baby. I don't have the strength or courage to go through this again."

I was scheduled for another ultrasound the next day. When I arrived, I knew that God was with me and was working on my behalf. While the technician was looking at the ultrasound, she was mystified because she could not find a single tear in the placenta. The bleeding had stopped and God was moving mightily on our side.

My doctor was astonished but quite happy with the outcome. The bleeding had completely stopped and I had no more pain. We were then able to put the Shirodkar suture in at twelve weeks. I spent a lot of the time on bedrest and hospital stays but made it through.

Returning to Trinidad in 1988, for my wedding to John

At thirty-eight weeks, my beautiful daughter Christie-Ann was born in 1991 weighing six pounds, ten ounces. I was just as sick as the previous pregnancy and spent many weeks in the hospital, but I was doing much better because God answered my prayers. He heard my heart's cry and gave me this beautiful child.

Christie-Ann was a beautiful fair-skinned baby girl with big beautiful bright eyes and pink lips. I had an emergency cesarean section and I was not able to see my daughter for hours after she was born. My parents and sisters came to visit and they told me all about her. They mentioned how beautiful and alert she was.

A few hours later, the nurse brought her to me and I was completely in love. She was a bright spot in our life. We finally had our baby! Christie-Ann is the first grandchild on both sides and was thoroughly spoilt by her grandparents, aunts and uncles. The day we brought her home from the hospital stands out in my mind for two reasons. Firstly, it was the day that George H. W. Bush invaded Kuwait. Secondly, there was a massive snow storm. I was so scared because I wondered what kind of world this child would grow up in.

Christie thrived and was so smart. I knew she could be anything that she put her mind to. I went back to work when she was just three months old. I had to go on maternity leave early because of complications with the pregnancy. It was hard leaving her with my aunt but I knew she was well taken care of. I loved her so much. Her paternal grandmother came to visit us when Christie was four months old and by the time we looked around again, I was expecting. This pregnancy was just as before, in and out of hospital with a suture at twelve weeks. I was able to eat a little bit better with Joseph and gained a lot of weight with him. I was given a medication called Gravol to take, and this helped with the vomiting. I still suffered with intense nausea but was able to keep some food down because of the medication.

My husband had to go out of town for work and the day he left, I went into labor. I was thirty-three and a half weeks pregnant and scared as ever. The doctor tried for two days to stop my contractions, but after some testing, they decided to do another cesarean section and I delivered a son in 1992. Joseph was actually a big baby for his gestational age and he was fair and resembled my father. We had another beautiful soul in our care. My family surrounded us and my mother-in-law was with us and helped me with the kids, until my husband returned from his job. Life was tough, financially, and it was hard. We had to depend on our relatives for some of our basic needs. But God took us through every single storm we encountered!

Things started to pick up and we were able to make ends meet.

During this period, we were going through the immigration process to become permanent residents in Canada and we had to move in with my parents for a little while to help with the cost of lawyers and immigration fees. My husband got some horrible counselling from our then pastor. He told him, not to move in with my parents and this caused more tension in our marriage. Why would you, a man of God, give such advice to the people that worship under your ministry? We had nowhere else to go and staying with another church member was not an option for me.

My parents were also a part of his congregation. I also realized that I was pregnant again and had to start the whole process, once more. The pregnancy was as usual, hard and also my son Joseph was very ill. One Sunday evening, Joseph became very sick; we had to take him to the emergency room. He had a high fever and was very congested. At one point, he just became lifeless in my arms. The tears were just streaming down my face and I kept praying for God to do something. My prayer was, *"Lord, please don't make him die. I love him so much."*

He was admitted to the hospital and was diagnosed with asthma and bronchitis. Eventually, he was released and we always had to give him inhalers of steroids and Ventolin. But God brought us through this time again. There was something special about this baby, but he cried a lot and sometimes, I didn't know what to do. I would pick him up and sing to him about the blood of Jesus and he would become quiet and sometimes just fall asleep. I know that God has a call on his life to do great things for him. I felt that I cared about him more than anyone else, even his dad. I would keep him with me all the time. This little boy needed me and I made sure to be there for him.

In the summer of 1993, after being in labor for almost a month on and off, my baby boy, Christopher was born. Christopher was a little darkie as we called them in the islands, so cute with his full head of curls. He was our surprise package. All of the kids were born a year apart. God blessed us with generally healthy children. It was not easy but they were worth all the pain and heartache I had to endure. I love these three with all my heart and I would not change a single thing about having them.

Having three babies all under the age of two was incredibly hard, especially when they were sick. One spring all the kids were sick. Each one diagnosed with asthma and had to be hospitalized. I could not drive and our car was parked in the garage. It was on one of those days I vowed to get my driver's license and I did that when Christopher was ten months old. My brother's wife, Desta was a great help to us during those times. She would stay at the hospital while I would go home and sleep. I will always remember her love and care for my family and continue to pray that God would bless her.

Christie-Ann, Christopher and Joseph ( My babies)

My youngest son Christopher and I

My son Joseph and I

Christie-Ann and I ( My minnie me)

~Chapter Five~

Making Memories

After being married for twenty-five years, there were moments that I fondly remember. We travelled to Pennsylvania to visit family at Christmas and it was a beautiful time. Our children enjoyed those moments, seeing the snow on the trees, as we drove along those long winding highways through New York, Christmas carols playing and just the peaceful atmosphere, in the vehicle. Sometimes, that silence was golden. We were not thinking about the struggles we were having but making sure we gave our kids some great childhood memories. There were songs and sights that even today they remember fondly. Our youngest child Christopher loved Barney so we would play that a lot, and the others kids love Disney music as well as children's Christian songs.

John was always good at taking us to sights and places in and around our province. Niagara Falls, African Lion Safari, Centre Island and many times to see fireworks around the July first celebrations.

He taught the kids to ride their bicycle, roller skate and tie their shoelaces. He was a good father, especially in their very early years.

We travelled to our homeland when the kids were babies so that they could meet their paternal grandad, aunts, uncles and many cousins. These were pleasant times and those times, I truly tried to be the best wife I could be. Although many times I felt that I was never good enough.

I remember traveling with the church. We travelled across the United States and Canada singing and being a support to the ministers who were the speakers for the meeting. I made a lot of great connections and friends that I am still in touch with today. A few times, my husband travelled with us and it was nice to do so, as we did not travel together very often. Church was a very important part of our life and sometimes caused us some stress as well.

We continued to struggle in our marriage, never fighting outwardly but we just could not seem to move past whatever was holding us apart. Life was not fun at all. We would have some really nice times but happiness was always fleeting.

Our tenth year anniversary was coming up and I decided to plan a Niagara Falls getaway for us. My girlfriend Cindy lived with us and she stayed with our children. I invited another couple to go with us and we had a really good time. We went across to Buffalo, New York, had lunch and just enjoyed the sights and the sound of the place. I loved planning things like this to break up the everyday routines. Sometimes, it would be with the kids, as well. Whatever I could do to help our lives be better, I tried. It worked for a while but it would always go back to the silence and disappointments.

We were both lonely in the marriage. My husband became silent and communication was almost nonexistent between us. Physically, we were Ok but there was no harmony in our marriage. I felt that nothing I did, made him happy and the weight of having the kids so close together was hard. I cried many days and night. I needed to immerse myself in trying to raise them. During this time, and really throughout our marriage, books were a constant companion. I have read hundreds of books because I could escape in the pages of my book and create my own reality of what I wanted in life.

In the year two thousand, my in-laws sent for our kids to come visit them in Trinidad for the summer holidays, and I decided to go with them for their vacation.

Thus another chapter began in my life.

Three Generations Of Women.
My Mother Maria Caprietta, Christie-Ann and Myself

The Kids in Trinidad (2000)

~Chapter Six~

# A Bad Decision

There's an old adage that says, if we don't close the doors to the past, it will often come back to haunt us later, when you least expect it. As I soon came to realize, there was a lot of truth in this statement.

I was travelling with the kids and we had an enjoyable experience spending time with their aunts, uncles and cousins. I was on vacation for two weeks. We went to the beach with my in-laws, it was awesome. I saw my kids just being kids, building sandcastles and swimming with their uncle. It was just beautiful to see them enjoying our homeland. My girlfriend Nicki and her husband took us to the zoo and again the children just enjoyed it. The days were sunny and warm. The climate was just right. To see my children playing in the rain and having fun finding bugs and building a fort in their grandparents drain was a delight for me.

My daughter got a fungus on her feet and I took her to the hospital clinic to get it looked after. Who would I meet after fifteen years? Yes, you guessed it. Dr. Orin. He was the one who had invaded my dreams and my heart for so many years. The last thing I wanted to do, was keep the flames of passion alive but because I left the door slightly open, my heart leapt for joy, as all of the old emotions came flooding back. I felt angry at first and I had so many questions.

*"Why didn't he fight for me, when I left Trinidad?"*

*"Why did he not want me to have our child?"*

The fact that he was not upfront with me about himself and left many things hidden in the dark, was an unresolved issue and I wanted closure. However, none of that ever really mattered because I was a married woman. I couldn't go back now.

I tried really hard not to let my feelings overwhelm me but the pull was so strong, it took my breath away. Doc was very nice and respected the fact that I was married and had three children.

We stayed in touch after I returned home. I was smitten and felt like a school girl all over again. One of the many things I played over and over in my head was why I had not mentioned it to my husband at the time. Doc came up for a medical conference to Toronto. We went out together and I did not tell my husband about it. We spent an amazing day touring the University of Toronto and having lunch. Just catching up. I was in my own world, forgetting that I was married.

Sometimes, you think that a relationship has to be physical, to be illicit or adulterous. The fact that you are spending more time with someone of the opposite sex other than your spouse and telling them all your desires, dreams and wishes; is cheating. You are outside your bounds and you are violating your marriage vows. Even if you are not physically involved, especially for a woman, your heart becomes involved; you are having an affair. You hide the calls , text messages and emails and you're smiling more or dressing differently. These are signs of what's happening with you and your relationship.

My husband finally became aware of this and a bad situation became unbearable. I was someone singing in the church choir, the wife of a deacon and finding myself facing this kind of situation. It was one of the darkest times in my life.

It is always best to close those doors to the past. There is a saying, "That it is easy for old fire sticks to catch fire." I regret being so foolish. I tried with all my heart to not go in that direction, but I had someone to talk with and who made me feel beautiful and alive again.

After this situation, my husband and I tried to put the pieces of our lives back together, but were not able to do so, successfully. I guess the hurt and pain it caused to my husband, brought out the worst in us. I was never made to forget what happened. There were constant reminders whenever an argument came up and it was hard to live with. I tried to conform and do all that I could but it was never enough. I did not apologize enough or I still had an independent streak and made decisions without discussing with him. We renewed our vows and tried to put the past behind us but it was not easy.

One day, I found myself not wanting to come out of the bed and at this time, my blood pressure was very unstable. It would become really high and I started taking medication to control it. The one thing that kept me going was reading. I would lie in bed and read. It would sometimes take me a couple hours to read a novel and I would pick up another one. I loved romance novels and then I found Christian novels and bought them all the time. Reading the Christian novels started giving me hope and in almost everyone I read, there was a message that was speaking to my situation. There were two authors that really helped me, Karen Kingsbury and Francine Rivers. Their stories were crafted in the word of God and I started hearing the whispers of my father, "For I know the plans I think towards you saith the lord"; over and over again. It helped me to learn more of God's word.

Some days, the stress was so palpable; I did not know what to do. While I was lying on the bed one afternoon, I started praying and I asked God to please speak to me. With an audible voice I heard, *"Go read Judges 5 verse 12."* The passage read *"Awake, awake, Deborah: awake, awake, and utter a song:"*

I opened my eyes and I sat on the floor. After reading it, I just bawled, the tears were streaming down my face. The God of heaven spoke to me through his word. He *knew* my name.

I have read the bible and the book of Judges. Seeing my name as plain as day confirmed a deep truth in my life. God is real and throughout my life, I have experienced his love and mercy.

My marriage was not the only struggle, I had to face. Six months after we bought our first home, We had a friend stay with us. This gentleman was one of my father's spiritual sons from our church in Trinidad. He had just split up from his wife and stayed in our basement. I thought this was going to be a temporary situation but it turned into five and a half years. While staying in our home, he remarried and brought his new wife and five children to live with him. I was happy to help to help them because I knew his new wife, but after a while I had to endure disrespect from him and his wife. Many times, I walked on eggshells in my own home.

Our home had one bathroom and thirteen people to share it. It was chaotic to say the least. The sad part was that I had no one to stand up for me in our home. My husband made me feel like I was the bad person who did not show love to others. I bore the pain and my body reacted to all this stress in a negative way. God kept me and eventually they moved out. I have always had a heart that desired to help others. If someone needed a place to stay, our door was always open. That was our life and service to people in need.

We sold our home just four months later. Over the course of the past few years, I have seen him and it's sad to say that their marriage did not last. It hurt to see how most of the young people that I knew from the old days at church, have suffered broken marriages, some multiple times.

~Chapter Seven~

# Going Beyond The Affair

*Prov.3:5-5 "Trust in the Lord with all your heart, And lean not on your own understanding; In all your ways acknowledge Him, And He shall direct your paths."*

In two-thousand and three, we sold our first house and bought a newly built home. This was exciting, as we watched it being built and got to choose all of the fixtures, cabinetry and flooring to go in our new home. When we closed the deal and got our keys, we took our children , held hands in a circle and prayed that God would bless it and that we would have a great life there. We were very optimistic. Life appeared to be going in the right direction, finally. Our children seemed okay and life was quiet for a time. I got laid off a month after we moved in, but I kept looking for a job and found one just before Christmas. We had family visiting and life seemed calm. We took a family vacation and went to Disney World. We also travelled to Myrtle Beach, with my two girlfriends and our daughters. We left the men in Myrtle Beach and went on a short cruise to the Bahamas. It was fun.

We had an amazing time. My father in-law was on this trip and he really enjoyed himself. This would be the last family trip we took and the only time, he travelled with us. It cost us a great amount of money; but as I reflect on it, it was great for our children to spend this time with their grandfather. I made sure everyone had a good time and will never regret it.

I continued to work as a Lab Technician and just kept going about my daily grind. Life was a challenge and I was driving up to eight hours a day, working in the community. One morning, I was on my way to a retirement home. As I approached the house, I started to feel like I could not breathe and my head and my heart were pounding. I began to black out behind the wheel. I knew I had to get help. I pulled over and called 911.

I barely made it to the home before I passed out. I was rushed to the emergency room. After much testing they found a small tumor on my brain. I did CT scans and MRI's but thanks to God, it was not cancer. After this, however, I struggled with anxiety. I went to see a psychiatrist to find out how I could relieve the symptoms of anxiety. I was given two different drugs, one was Ativan. Whenever I felt anxious, I would rush to have one under my tongue, so the feeling would subside. What I did not realize is that I was becoming addicted to the meds. In order to feel calm I started to increase the dosage. When it was finished, I wondered how I could get more. I lived with this for over four years.

One day, I had to travel to Buffalo, New York Airport to pick up my aunt. My mom came along with me. During our drive, I could not sit still because there were tractor trailers that felt like they were closing in on us. The anxiety was so bad, I cried many times for God to help me. I told my mom what was happening with me and she began to pray, while driving. I could feel the presence of God surround me and the intensity, the anxiety began to diminish. Even till this day, whenever I am driving on the highway, I would still feel a little nervous. However, it is not as bad as it was. Sometimes, I don't even notice these feelings, unless the other people in traffic are not driving correctly.

There were other times, I saw God in action in my life. July 1st, 2001, our family was on a trip to Harrisburg, Pennsylvania and for some reason, I just felt lethargic.

This trip took just about eight hours and it was a trip we made several times, but this time, it was different. We arrived at our relative's home and it was a regular hot summer day. I just wanted to sleep and could not shake the feeling that something was not right. One of my cousins called and as I was speaking with her, I happened to look at my face in the bathroom mirror; to my surprise, it looked like it was twisted to the right. Alarmed, I called my sister-in-law and immediately, I was rushed to the emergency room. Having been diagnosed with hypertension, we were terrified that I was having a stroke.

I was there for a few hours, just making sure it was not a stroke. The doctors ruled out stroke but could not figure out at the time what it was. We travelled back to Canada and were met by my new doctor, who quickly diagnosed me with Bell's Palsy.

At this time, I had no idea what this disease was. I was of course terrified because I looked awful and felt bad, as well. The doctor gave me *Prednisone* to manage and sent us off to a neurologist. I was told that it would take about six to nine months to be healed but could have some residual effects. It just kept getting worse. The next night, there was a church service, so we went to church and there was a visiting minister from France that had a gift of healing. So when the prayer line was called, I went up to be prayed for.

The minister asked what was wrong and after telling him what the doctor told me, he said, "The doctor told you six months before you are better but I tell you it will be six days."

With this renewed faith, I believed and trusted the word spoken to me. It was exactly six days from Tuesday to Sunday and when I went to church on that Sunday, I sang a song and gave a testimony of God's healing power. If you see me today you would never know that I had once suffered with Bell's Palsy. God healed me, completely.

Over the years, I have experienced a lot of illness and stress. My health was challenged and at times I did not know what to do. I was diagnosed with hypertension and diabetes and became very overweight. The one thing that kept me going was my faith in God. No matter what was happening around me, I never gave up. Knowing that my savior was always with me, was the greatest motivation.

Having a strong Christian upbringing, gave me the courage to keep smiling through my pain. My children were growing up and there were times, they made me cry because they were teenagers and going through the struggles of their hormonal years. The boys started drinking heavily and even experimented with smoking. I felt we were failing them because of our lack of communication and the tension in the home.

My three children gave me a lot of joy. We travelled everywhere together, church camps and singing all over the USA with our family band, 'Morningstar Voices.' Those were some of the happiest times for me, being on the road with my family, mother, father, siblings and my children. While we were out singing and ministering, the Lord was working on the hearts of the people that we met. There were people getting healed and delivered from many illnesses and situations. Wherever we went, people would always say, "The power of God was felt and seen in the place tonight."

The secret to our success as a group was that we always prayed together. We would fast once or twice a week, especially when we had an upcoming event. My sister Ruth, the band manager, called us to consecration for a period of time. Our family band was a dream, my father had and he lived to see his children singing and ministering all over North America, Canada and the Caribbean.

One of my younger brothers became the pastor of our local church and as we all attended this church, we grew in faith and came to really understand the nature of God.

Life started to change. I did not look as sad, as I had before. During this time, there were other changes on the horizon. I grew up in a church organization that was very legalistic and sometimes oppressive when the opportunity arose. I left that church and went to my brother's church. This was the beginning of the end for my family unit, as we knew it. My husband felt disrespected because we did not go to the church together anymore.

At Bethel, I felt that I had a sense of purpose; I was part of the worship team and was making a difference where I was. With all this happening, life in our home was becoming more and more strained. My husband and I argued all the time. We were not operating as a unified family. The stress and tension was so thick, you could cut it with a knife. Finances were bad and to top it off, I was laid off from my job as a Laboratory Assistant. We almost lost our home and we were able to pull it together but the interest was very high, causing us more pressure. It was during this period, I went back to school to study Event and Venue Management; and because finances were not the best, I spent some days during the week in the city, so I could save some money for our family. I would make sure on a weekend that food was cooked for a few days and the laundry was done.

My husband was very withdrawn and he said he was taking a vacation back to Trinidad to visit with family. I was happy for him. His parents were there and I felt it was good for him to get away. His leaving this time, however, was different. I would normally take him to the airport but on this trip, our son did. When he arrived, he would always call to let us know he arrived and this did not happen. It was strange and I kept trying to contact him but to no avail. I travelled to New York with my sister, to sing at a conference and during that time, our home was on the market and I needed to contact him. He eventually texted me and I gave him the information, which was needed to accept or decline the offer. That was the only communication in three weeks. I knew that something was not right and decided to ask questions with no real answers. So I decided to start searching for any clues and I found it. With my heart pounding, I tried calling him at work and after leaving a message, he finally called me back. He was having an affair and was leaving. I was in college and the days I had to travel from Oshawa to Toronto on the GO Train, I would be crying and trying to figure out how I was going to cope with all that was happening in our lives. We had our teenage kids who were confused and angry.

*How do we navigate this storm that just blew into their lives.*

This question was constantly present in my thoughts. It was hard but we did it.

I can finally say that, *"Through the storms and through the night, the Lord held my hand."*

Within thirty days, our home was sold. The day we closed on the sale of our home was the day we separated for good. Two of my great friends from school, kept me sane. Carol and Tamara took me under their wings and we helped each other during those tough days. I went to live with my friend and sister, Cindy, who was at one time more like a daughter to me. She helped me out for about a month and then we were able to get an apartment for myself and the kids to live.

~Chapter Eight~

# Separation

**Psalms 34:19** *"The righteous person may have many troubles, but the LORD delivers him from them all;"*

No one gets married with the intention of getting divorced. The decision to go in separate directions, is often a challenging and painful experience. Having been married for twenty-five years and struggling for most of those years, the decision to end the marriage was still a difficult one.

*"What will people think about us?"*

*"Will they believe I have failed my family?"*

These thoughts persisted in the back of my mind.

Even though we had known the marriage was over for a long time, the decision to end the marriage was still a hard process. The outcome of this experience left me feeling emotionally drained, as I grappled with a deep sense of loss and regret. The problems we faced were obvious to our families and friends. Why did we wait so long? Often when there are children in a marriage people tend to hold on.

The questions became, *"Do I stay for the children or do we end it now?"*

No one can answer that question for you but yourself. For me, I chose to stay because I did not want to be a statistic and I wanted the children to grow up with their father.

One of the lessons I have learned is that by staying married, we did not do our children any favors. They now have a much skewed vision of marriage and relationships.

My sons are afraid to get married but our daughter knows exactly what she wants in a marriage, even really allowing her husband to take the lead but also being a part of the decision-making for their family. I must say I have seen God working on my boys and their views on marriage, however small that might be.

For anyone making this life changing decision, a lot of thought goes into it. The choice to separate or divorce, has long lasting repercussion for you and your family. Ending a marriage is like a death in your family and we know that no one is happy when someone in your family dies. It was evident that our marriage was not working from early into it but because of our strong religious background, we decided to stay and try to make it work. We didn't want to separate six months into our marriage, even though this was how early we knew that we were in trouble.

You may ask me, "why did you stay in the marriage for twenty-five years?

To be honest, I don't have the answer to that question. After our children were born, we wanted them to have a family that was united, mum, dad and the children.

After going through turbulence in marriage, life can really beat you down and a lot of illnesses and complications can happen, as was the case in our family.

Just after celebrating our twenty-fifth wedding anniversary, we decided to seek counselling, which my husband was very opposed to for all those years but decided to do so. However, he agreed to it, not willingly but to humor me. It was a complete failure! Two months later, we were talking about separation.

When our marriage encountered infidelity for a second time, it became the final straw that literally broke the remainder of the foundation. We were not able to salvage the remains of our relationship and this eventually ended the marriage. It was very devastating because now we were forced to make decisions with a third party in the equation. It would not be fair to the burden this other individual with blame. I will only say that it complicated the situation further.

Infidelity changes the dynamics of one's marriage. Not only does it inflict pain on your partner and it is also harmful to yourself. It is always so much better to keep other people out of your marriage. Sometimes, due to feeling of being alone, you will turn to someone else. Infidelity usually occurs when there is some need that has not been met and in order to fulfill this desire, the temptation to turn to another person can seem like the ultimate fix. However, this sense of satisfaction is fleeting and does not last long. Marriage is hard work, it requires you to extend grace to the other person during their lowest points and vice versa. What makes an affair so attractive is that there is very little commitment required. An affair of any kind thrives on fantasy. It is a form of escapism that allows the individual to emotionally and mentally remove themselves from the reality of their situation. If you or your partner find yourself grappling with effects of an affair, this does not mean you are a bad person, but you have made a wrong choice which has lasting consequences.

If someone were to ask me if I loved my husband, I would always say yes because it was true or vice versa, but in many cases, love is just not enough. We think so many times, "If I love you, things will get better." For some, that would actually hold true.

Life happens and then there is a runaway train on the tracks with an accident waiting to happen. That was us!

This book is about my experience; having gone through the situation and having a few really good friends go through it, made me think about writing this book.

I realized that faced with so many emotions during this time of transition and knowing how to navigate them was a learning curve for the children and me.

These are some of the emotions you go through during the time of separation and could be compounded during divorce. One of the things that kept occurring during my early days of separation was meeting many women who were going through a separation or divorce. As we began talking, I began to realize a pattern and similarities in our lives - the brokenness and anger, the feeling of loss and low self-esteem.

The main thing for me was, why was I not good enough? I loved you and you said you loved me, but we could not work together in harmony, why? Why did you criticize me instead of celebrating me? I gave you the children being so sick almost to the point of death and you just became silent towards me, why? As you can see, I had so many questions and really no answers. Please don't get me wrong, I made my share of mistakes and the breakdown of a relationship is never one person, it's both parties.

I could look back and see where I also went wrong, I was so lonely during my marriage. I had friends and relatives but the joy and confidence that I should have had with my husband was not there at all. Towards the end of our marriage, I became very angry and disillusioned.

I would book trips with my singing group and tell my husband the day before because it was always a sore point. I was afraid of the arguments and always feeling that I was doing something wrong, even though I was singing for the Lord. This type of action, caused more problems for me and our family. I think the biggest blow was choosing to walk away from our church of over thirty years because I saw the errors in the doctrine and the way the women were treated and I wanted no part of it.

Religion played a big part in the marriage, and don't get me wrong, I love God and respect His word but I dislike religion. It causes wars, family separation and a whole lot of problems. Money or money management is also another part that can help or cause problems in a marriage. This topic adds complications and conflicts. Therefore, if you are considering getting married, you would definitely want to have great conversations about money matters before going into marriage. When we realized that the marriage was not going to work and finally, it was time to separate, life became a maze to go through. The truth be told, I was in school because my job became redundant and I was laid off. So splitting up, with no real income and selling our home, made for real devastation.

I was fearful about what would happen, where the children and I would live and how was I supposed to survive this? I had no income except a small student loan to live on. Our two eldest children were in college and it was a really scary time.

Thankfully, we found an apartment and my husband supported us until I did my internship and honestly I am not sure how I passed my course.

I was able to secure two internships, a catering company and a media company. I worked these two internships and both companies were aware that I was going through a rough time and so they both made it a paid internship. I was hired on a contract at the media company and stayed on part time with the caterer. My father in heaven was looking out for me. At the media company, I worked hard and I have met many influential people. The praises would come from many of the patrons from the events we put on, but God kept me humble. After a while, I felt closed in and so frustrated living where we did, I decided to leave the country.

In April, 2015, I got on an airplane and flew to my native country, Trinidad and Tobago. The first month, I was just trying to get my head and heart together, yet not quite sure what to do. I had thoughts that I could probably see where the relationship with my first love would go and so in that moment I felt like I had a plan. We spent time just casually and it was nice, someone to talk to because I was starved for that male attention.

I learned that you have to love yourself and not be so needy of having someone to validate who you are.

Eventually, I began to have serious doubts about being in this relationship because it was not bringing joy, but pain. There were amazing trips and lunches and drives through the city but underneath, I could feel the rage because of the past. The conversation about my having kids that should have been his and also being blamed for me leaving and not coming back.

After what I experienced, I began pulling away from the relationship and closing my heart to everyone that was male. I felt I had to protect my heart and myself.

*When you have gone through a broken marriage or relationship, your mind can do strange things. My heart was broken and my feelings were that of rejection.*

I felt rejection from both my ex-husband, and my first love. This almost kept me in bondage, thinking I was not good enough and had me sticking around, where I stood a very big chance of being badly hurt. But my God kept me.

It was during that time, I formulated a plan to help myself get out of my rot. For one thing, I made sure that when I was dressed, I looked and felt beautiful. I was getting a lot of attention and it felt nice to be desirable again. With all this, I made sure to keep myself from getting entangled with anyone.

My Christian values were still intact, and I wanted above all, to serve God.

I found myself a job and in six months moved out of my aunt's home. I found a beautiful apartment in a gated community. Wow! This was the absolute first time, I had ever been alone in my life. I grew up with six siblings, left my country and lived with my grandparents and my aunts all living at home. Married from my parents' home, lived with my husband and children till then. For the first forty-six years of my life, I was cocooned, surrounded by people whom I knew.

I was so scared, but determined to put on my big girl 'panties' and take charge of my life.

I found a new job in my field as a Laboratory Technician and started in the New Year.

In October of 2015, I came home to Canada, to work on two award shows that I was contracted for, The Excellence Awards and in November, the Canada Glass Awards.

The bible tells us; *"For I know the plans I have for you,"* declares the Lord, *"plans to prosper you and not to harm you, a plan to give you hope and a future." (Jeremiah 29:11).*

During the busy sessions for the awards, I had no time to think about my troubles. I was working and feeling happy because travelling back and forth from the Caribbean was giving me that sense of freedom; "Girl, you can do this, living that life." I spent time with my children and grandson, parents and siblings. The feeling of strength and accomplishment was real and I began to see the changes in myself.

My confidence was coming back and my head was held a little higher. I still had my moments of utter depression and sadness but at least there was progress.

The Excellence Awards came and it went very well. One week later, *The Glass Awards* was took place. *The Canada Glass Awards* is a gospel music award show that awards excellence in the Christian music community and helps to mentor up-and-coming artist in Canada.

Working on the Media and Red Carpet for this show was interesting and quite time consuming but we pulled it off with class.

The Excellence Awards

## November 4th 2015, Glass Awards

My beautiful daughter, Christie-Ann and her boyfriend, were attending the Glass Awards and they looked incredible. That evening she brought a good friend of hers to meet me. This was a gentleman who had lived in our old neighbourhood. We had never met, but our children were friends. To be honest, I was busy and just had enough time to say hello. At the end of the evening, I once again encountered her guest and we had a short conversation. He took photos of my daughter and I, and of course, we took photos together.

We chatted for a little while and he left, while I continued closing up the event.

My flight was leaving on Monday evening for Trinidad so I really had no time to chat or socialize with anyone. However, I got a call from Mr. Wright. He was just checking to see when I was leaving and he was a little disappointed that I was leaving so soon. We exchanged phone numbers and I left on my trip.

To be quite honest, I was not looking for anything or anyone, but God has his own plans for each and every one of us. I arrived in Trinidad and promptly found an apartment and this is where I found myself. It is in the lonely hours of the night, when it's you and God alone; you can call upon him and be ready to listen to what he has to tell you. I would play the Christian radio all through the night because

I was not comfortable living alone, as yet. It was now my reality to be in another country away from my family. It was during those times, I could talk to God. In my normal way of life, I am a social butterfly. I loved entertaining and having lots of company but in this season, my home was my sanctuary. I was very protective of who entered into my space. On Christmas day, Orin came over to share breakfast and lunch with me and left so early that I was all alone on Christmas day after 2 pm. I missed my children, my adorable grandson and my big happy family. I vowed never to do that again.

New Year's Eve night, I prayed and thanked god for the coming year and then I cried myself to sleep. At midnight, I heard a loud bang and felt like there were rocks falling on my roof. I jumped up only to realize that it was fireworks going off. I stayed on my back porch taking in the festivities and went back to bed.

My birthday is within the holiday season, therefore, on January 2nd, I celebrated my 49th birthday. This time was also a big disappointment. I had no one to celebrate it with. I visited a dear person to me, who was very ill and that was my father-in-law. He passed, six days later. We lost my aunt the day after him and our world was in mourning. Mom and Dad came to Trinidad for the funerals and stayed with me. It was actually the first time my parents stayed with me in my home. Mom told me how very proud she was of me, finding some peace and looking so happy. This made me feel a little more whole.

My children flew in for their grandad's funeral and my girlfriend, Tamara also flew in to be with me and my family.

After all the funerals, I decided to take my children and Tamara on a mini vacation to our twin Island, Tobago. We got on the Ferry, a two and a half hour ride to Tobago. I arranged a rental car and a villa owned by my cousin. With all the sadness now behind us, we awoke to the sounds of birds chirping. We had our coffee on the porch, just enjoying the sights and sounds of the Caribbean. We packed up and headed for the beach and took a trip to the famous Bucco Reefs and Nylon Pool, where the kids were able to take their mind off of the pain of losing Grandpa. It worked like magic and we had an awesome time. Having Tamara there with us was like a "balm in Gilead."

When we returned to Trinidad, I had to go back to work and Tamara assisted my parents. She made breakfast and made sure that they were Ok. My father had been diagnosed with Parkinson's disease, a few years prior and it was great for my mom to have the extra help. God Bless her heart.

Life continued on but I started to get a little restless and lonesome for home.

After I moved into my own apartment, I had to change where I went to church. The previous church were really nice because I found out one of my dear friends from college, pastored that church and I stayed there for a while. However, it was difficult for me to get to his church after the move and God enabled me to find another place of worship. I enjoyed it and started leading worship. I was learning to live again. Best of all, I was happy once again, smiling and enjoying life.

We have to know when to sit still and let God lead us, and at this church, I could also feel the stirrings of the call on my life to be in ministry. I was not sure where or in what capacity because I was always been a worshipper but this was different.

My heart started yearning to do more with the women's ministry and I was not sure how to go about making that happen. God had a plan!

Meeting Carlton for the first time at
The Canada Glass Awards

The Canada Glass Awards

My children and grandson Roman ( 2015 )

The trip to Tobago after the Funeral

My grandson Roman

Dad and I

## April 7th, 2016

While cruising on Facebook I realized it was Carlton's birthday, so I sent him a happy birthday note and left it at that. A few days later, I sent him a message on WhatsApp and he responded. Hmmm, I thought to myself. We kept texting and the conversation was really interesting. This went on for about an hour. I said to him, "Would you like to chat instead?" He was agreeable and we had an amazing conversation. We promised to keep in touch and Carlton texted me the next morning.

I was a little stunned that we had so much in common, from our children our situations and even where we lived.

Carlton and I had an instant connection, this time around. We started talking every night, texting in the morning and really throughout the day. He was so attentive. I was six hours away in the Caribbean and it felt like he was just down the streets.

I kept working in Trinidad but without the children and my precious siblings. I was lonely. The late evenings and nights were great because Carlton and I were always talking. He made me laugh and think a lot. The similarities of our lives were really surreal. I have three children, two boys and a girl and he has the reverse two girls and a boy. We both separated from our previous spouses in August 2013 and sold our homes around the same time. We actually had the exact model of house in the same neighbourhood and never once met each other, living there for ten years. I found all those coincidences incredible.

My Aunt, Fannie and I had made a deal to stay in Trinidad and Tobago and live there for a while. When she arrived in Trinidad, she wanted to actually move to Tobago. So we started to pack up the apartment to make that move. I wanted to stay but my heart was now pulled back to Canada, wanting to explore the building of a relationship with Carlton. The apartment was packed up. Since it was a furnished apartment, it was just our personal belongings that had to be packed and stored.

We decided that I would come home to visit and see how things went from there. I arrived on June 1$^{st}$, 2016 and finally got to meet my sweetheart, for the first time.

Oh, my goodness, I could now see him in person and hold his hand! It was amazing!

We met at his bus station. He was so handsome and I felt my heart pounding because now I could see if what we were feeling was real. He hugged and kissed me for the first time. The stars were shining bright! The summer progressed and we had some really great times. I had to work at my annual show on June 4$^{th}$, and now, he was included. He helped me pick out my gown, a nice soft pink with a sheer fabric and lace. I felt like a princess. He wore a nice dark suit and a bowtie that complimented my dress. I was on top of the world. My friends and family were very curious to meet this man that had totally captured my heart and attention.

It was so funny that during this time, my daughter was having a hard time dealing with her mother dating someone, other than her father. She told me three years prior,

"Why don't you separate from my father, you guys are just miserable together." Now she was not speaking to her friend who was also like a dad to her, and barely to me. In other words, she was being a brat!

In August, Carlton told me to pack a bag for a day we were going to head to Kingston, Ontario to enjoy 1,000 Islands. I was so excited, nervous but excited. We told our family we were heading out; not that we might stay over as it was a good ways away and we wanted to do a long tour to the castle. We rented a car, packed up and headed to Gananoque, Ontario.

*~Chapter Eleven~*

***Courting***

*'Weeping may endure for the night but joy comes in the morning' Ps 30:5*

Carlton and I took our first trip together. I had never been on a trip with any man except my ex-husband and my family. This experience was unnerving but exciting. We travelled and we talked the whole way. Conversation was never stilted or awkward. Carlton and I were in sync with each other. He drove and I was his co-pilot, making sure that we stayed on course. I booked a hotel room for one night as the tour we wanted to go on left earlier than we arrived. We checked in, got changed and went out shopping and had an early dinner. Dinner that evening was in a quaint restaurant in Kingston, we tried some new foods and just enjoyed the ambience of the place.

We just had such a great time walking and getting to know each other. God was always a big part of our focus and attention and we knew that we would make sure that we honor those parameters that were set.

The next morning, we got up, did some devotions and set out for breakfast. After we ate, we booked our tour. We had the camera, passports and hats in hand. The morning was beautiful, warm and sunny. This was especially a good sign since we were going to travel on the Hudson River by ferry.

We followed the directions and arrived at our destination. I got our tickets and we boarded the ferry, *Uncle Sam*, in Clayton, Ontario.

The ride was very informative and pleasant. We saw many islands with some of the most interesting homes. There were two tours; one was a two hour trip along the river and back; the second was a five hour trip which included stopping at the famous Boldt Castle. It took about an hour and a half to reach the castle. on the American side of the islands, we had to go to the castle through the immigration procedure which was very quick.

We got off the ferry and went onto the castle grounds; it was really a nice place to visit. We saw the gardens, and some of the outer buildings then we had lunch and toured the castle. It had stained glass window ceilings, and the décor was kept to the time period when the castle was built. Carlton and I really enjoyed ourselves.

On the return ride, he said to me, "Babe pinch me."

I did and asked him, "Why?"

His reply was so profound to me that I stopped and just had to stare at him. "This is real? I thought I was dreaming."

This pulled at my heartstrings because I also felt the same way. This trip opened my eyes to the possibilities of our relationship. Even though, we were both previously married, there was lack in what we'd experienced. After our boat ride back from the castle, we decided to go across the US border to do some shopping, I set the navigator but upon our arrival, we slightly deviated from our plan and actually went into the little border town that was close to the river. It was beautiful. We had ice cream and listened to some music by the water. While sitting there, I wanted to take a selfie of us and an elderly couple stopped and took the picture for us. This picture captured us with the sun setting behind us.

With our relationship growing and flourishing, I got the courage to get back into doing my business. I started sharing about it to the people around me and also networking whenever I could.

We decided to do a Valentine's Day dinner and we worked as a team to pull it off. The event of itself went well, despite a massive snowstorm. My next goal was to get some weddings booked and we did. Now the confidence that I had lost was coming back. In our region, the government offers a program to assist small business owners and I applied and was accepted.

I kept working on myself and my business, but sometimes the negative thoughts would start returning, and the doubts would arise from time to time. However, I kept pushing through and silencing the voices. I now had encouragement and support to cushion the fear of stepping out.

I got a part-time job, which sometimes became a fulltime job and it was very rough but I needed to support myself and grow my business, so I kept going. My daughter got engaged at the Valentine's Day dinner and was married a few weeks later. I was happy for her and her new husband. My two younger sons were in their own relationships and seemed to be doing alright.

I just kept my hand to the plough and did what was

needed. During this time, I moved out of my girlfriend, Cindy's home and moved in with my parents. It was the best thing that I did for myself. I had the opportunity to spend time with them and help my mom with my father who had developed Parkinson's disease. This was a very rough time for our family. Dad was in and out of the hospital. It was very painful to see him deteriorate, the way he was.. Many days I cried, because my dad was a strong man, full of life. The most beautiful thing to see was the way, Mom took care of him. She was not rough or did anything for him, unwillingly. They honored the vows they took so many years ago

In sickness, and in health. They kept it. I admire them so much. They are my example of what a good marriage is.

In the spring of 2017, I decided to plan a birthday party for Carlton and enlisted the help of his sisters and his daughters. We had to do it secretly. I picked up the girls from the bus station, as they live about five hours away and brought them to the apartment to surprise their father. He had no clue and was most surprised.

I had to find a way to get him to the party, since it was in our building and gave the girls that task. We decorated and had everything all set. The family and friends were gathered and we were waiting on the guest of honor. I did this because during one of our many conversations, Carlton told me that he had never had a birthday party as an adult. I just wanted to wrap my arms around him because I could hear the longing in his voice.

He was surprised and had a great time. After the party, he was so thankful for it and it made me feel really happy.

Our journey continued and we were so in sync with each other. That summer was great. We spent a lot of time by the lake, out and about on some adventure or other. My family singing group was invited to Atlanta to sing at a concert, so we invited his girls to accompany us, as my daughter who was now married, could not just leave and travel with us, as before. She used to be my travel buddy. We had many great times on the road.

As we prepared for our journey, I had to go to the apartment and finish packing the travel bag for Carlton as he was still at work. Whilst packing, he came home, greeted me and we continued to get everything packed in the vehicle and finally get dressed to leave.

Carlton called out to me from the living room, I told him, I needed one minute and as I stepped out of the room, there he was holding a box with a beautiful ring. He held my hands, looked into my eyes and asked me to marry him. Of course, I said yes. I knew he was close to proposing, I just did not know when.

Carlton told me after that he had waited a while because he thought I wanted a big event for the proposal. I was surprised by this. He calls me a big celebrity and I always just laugh at this.

I called my family and his sister and told them the good news. I was happy that we were going to be partners for life. To work, play and grow old together. Our dreams and goals were so intertwined that we were amazed at the similarities. We started on our journey to Atlanta, stopping to pick up our girls and my aunt. Our family was really happy for us and so were the children. We drove fifteen hours to Atlanta and had an amazing time. This was the last trip my parents took with us. We spent time with my brother and his family in Atlanta then drove to Columbia, South Carolina to visit with our aunt and cousins. This was a very pleasant experience for us and for the girls as they had never been in the south before.

We travelled back to Windsor and my parents and aunt came with us. Carlton took such good care of my father. I think that was when my father fell in love with him. We spent time by the Detroit River, Dad was looking at people fishing, as this was something he loved doing but was now unable to do. The trip was great.

Coming back home was great, but now I had a wedding to plan in two months. This is my field, so I said, "No problem, I can do this." So we got our guest list, and as we wanted to keep the wedding small, I had to come up with a way to do just that. I discussed it with my mom and sisters and decided to have anyone who wanted to attend at the church. So we catered a cocktail reception for them and a private dinner for family and a few friends. The wedding was beautiful and as a gift to our children we included them in the ceremony by giving each one of them rings. The ladies have matching rings, which I picked out and the gentlemen the same.

Our wedding day was more than I could have ever imagined. The day was filled with joy, peace and love. The sun was shining with just a little bit of rain showers and a warm breeze. What I loved the most was that our families were happy for us, so there were no issues or fires to put out.

There was unity! God was in this and the enemy had to step aside. The feeling we had was that of peace and well-being. The love we shared and the peace we had after the turbulences, we've experienced, was well worth it to get to this moment. My hope in humanity was being restored and my heart was at peace. Planning and living a life with this man was a joy and something I wanted and needed. We settled into married life, as if it had been a lifetime; there was no awkwardness, we do most things together. When something is just right, you will know in your heart and you are able to really grow into your own. I have seen in my husband as we have spent time together praying, talking and planning what we want and where we're going, I know it is the hand of God working in us. The bible tells us that weeping may endure for the night but joy comes in the morning.

Our First Trip

Carlton And I

New Years Eve ( 2016)

Our Honeymoon

Honeymoon

Our Parents

Our Big Happy Family

Sisters

*Psalms 37:23 "The steps of a good man are ordered by the LORD: and he delighteth in his way." Psalms 37:24 "Though he fall, he shall not be utterly cast down: for the LORD upholdeth him with his hand."*

When I consider all the steps I've taken in my journey, it's incredible to realize just how far I have come. This memoir is not just about being married to Mr. Wright, but about me transforming into the most authentic version of myself. This is a story is about a woman called Debra who found the courage to walk in her own truths. Though, she has since acknowledged her mistakes and taken responsibility for her actions. She can't deny that every single moment has brought immeasurable growth in her life and she has is on a constant trajectory towards learning and exploring who she really is.

Along the way, she has had to go through the fire of sickness and divorce, anxiety and sometimes depression and is now able to stand in front of an audience and speak her truth. She is not ashamed of the mistakes she's made. Yes, she made them and worked through them. Regrets them, but she is not ashamed anymore.

There is one song that I recorded with our family band called *Refiners Fire*, I have sung this song so many times, not realizing that this was exactly what God was doing with me.

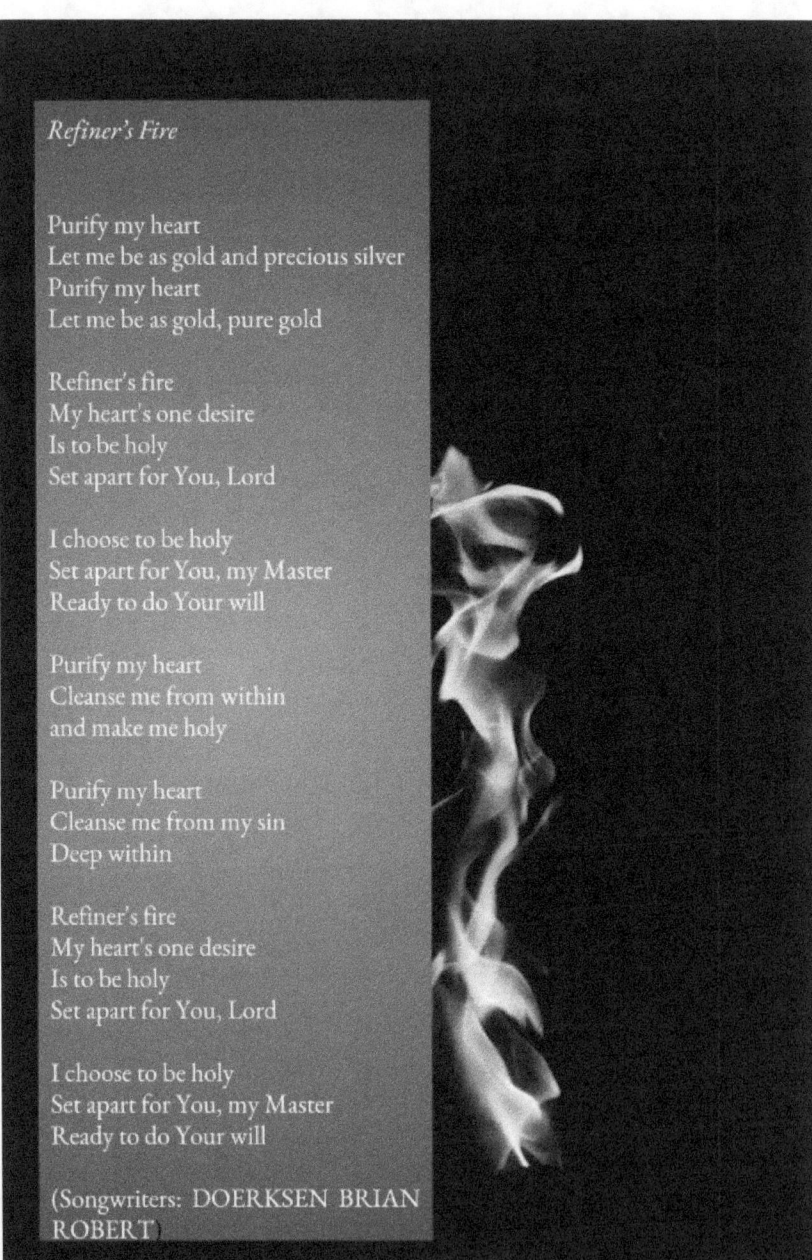

*Refiner's Fire*

Purify my heart
Let me be as gold and precious silver
Purify my heart
Let me be as gold, pure gold

Refiner's fire
My heart's one desire
Is to be holy
Set apart for You, Lord

I choose to be holy
Set apart for You, my Master
Ready to do Your will

Purify my heart
Cleanse me from within
and make me holy

Purify my heart
Cleanse me from my sin
Deep within

Refiner's fire
My heart's one desire
Is to be holy
Set apart for You, Lord

I choose to be holy
Set apart for You, my Master
Ready to do Your will

(Songwriters: DOERKSEN BRIAN ROBERT)

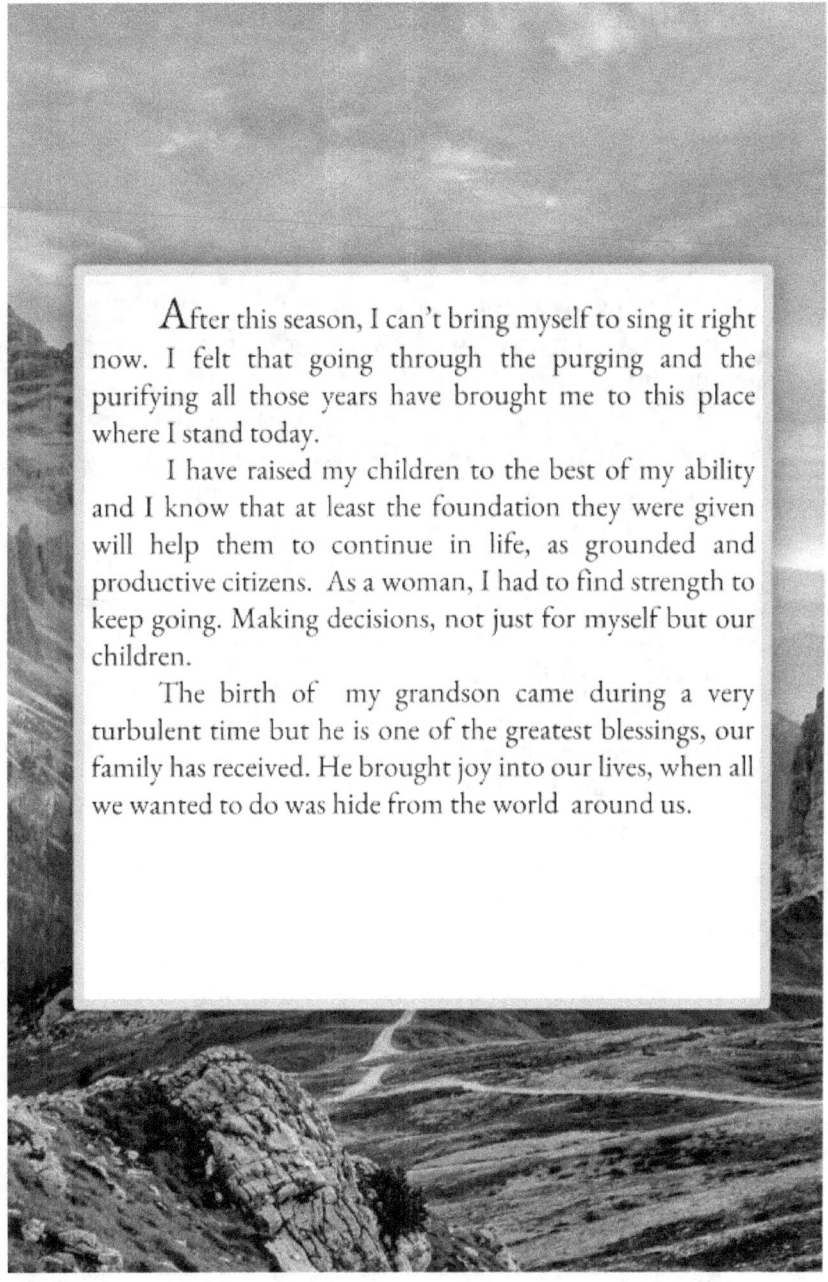

After this season, I can't bring myself to sing it right now. I felt that going through the purging and the purifying all those years have brought me to this place where I stand today.

I have raised my children to the best of my ability and I know that at least the foundation they were given will help them to continue in life, as grounded and productive citizens. As a woman, I had to find strength to keep going. Making decisions, not just for myself but our children.

The birth of my grandson came during a very turbulent time but he is one of the greatest blessings, our family has received. He brought joy into our lives, when all we wanted to do was hide from the world around us.

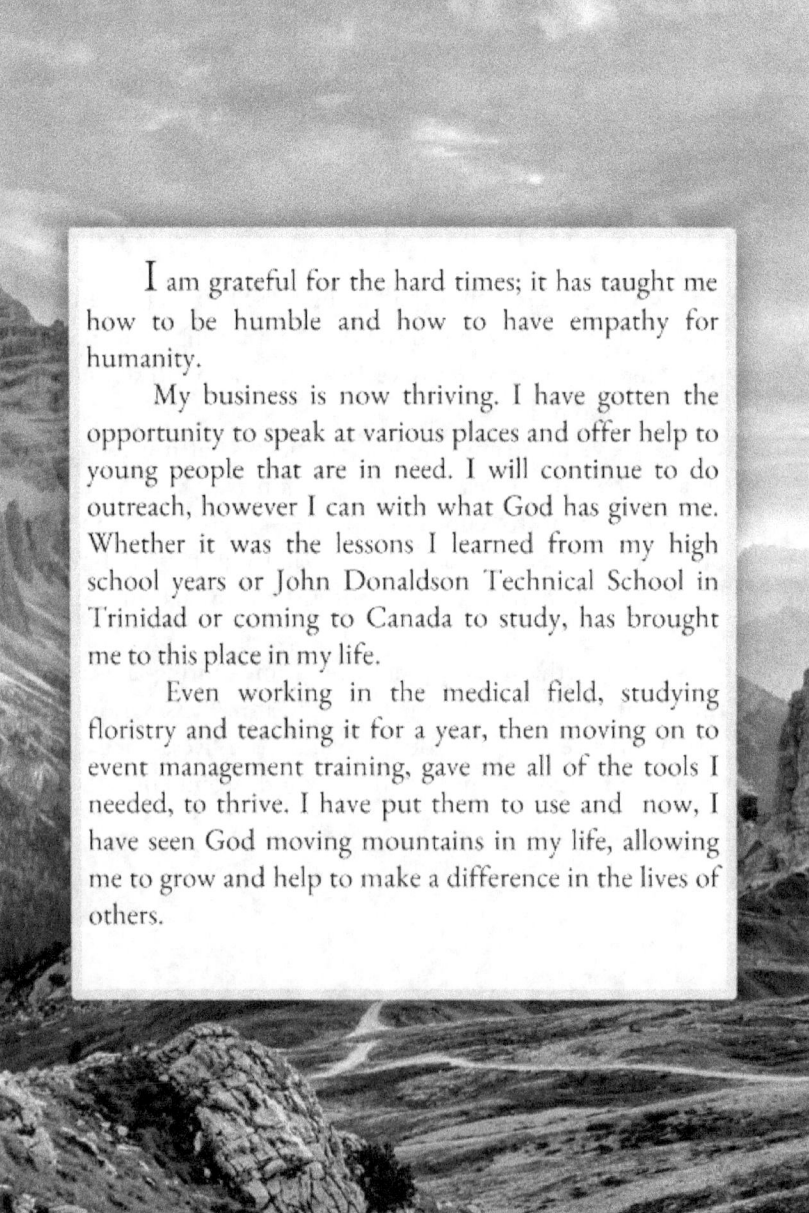

I am grateful for the hard times; it has taught me how to be humble and how to have empathy for humanity.

My business is now thriving. I have gotten the opportunity to speak at various places and offer help to young people that are in need. I will continue to do outreach, however I can with what God has given me. Whether it was the lessons I learned from my high school years or John Donaldson Technical School in Trinidad or coming to Canada to study, has brought me to this place in my life.

Even working in the medical field, studying floristry and teaching it for a year, then moving on to event management training, gave me all of the tools I needed, to thrive. I have put them to use and now, I have seen God moving mountains in my life, allowing me to grow and help to make a difference in the lives of others.

The love of oneself, should be able to propel you to be your best. The love of a good man or woman is a bonus and a blessing to your life. Your partner is not to complete you but to be a helpmate and companion on your life's journey. The life I now live is not a fairy tale one, but a real life, lived and still growing to become an even better and stronger person. I am a blessed woman. I have a great husband, six wonderful children and a grandson. Life is good.

# FINAL THOUGHTS

I am enjoying the partnership that I have with my husband, Carlton. Undoubtedly, retirement will soon be on the horizon and we are making concrete plans to prepare for it. We have a desire to travel across the world so that we can share the message of hope with God's people, no matter where they are. We are here in this world to be the salt and the light. With God's help, we will fulfill this mandate. All of our children are amazing and living in their own truth. We have given them a solid foundation and as we grow older, it is a joy to have our children and grandchildren around us. I want to share in their joys and triumphs, as we continue on this journey called life.

# EPILOGUE

I thank you for reading my memoir and I would like to leave this thought with you. On the pages of this book are some very heavy situations that transpired in my life, but through it all God has been my source and my strength. Some of you reading this book might be going through similar circumstances or even worse situations. Never give up!

There will always be a brighter day. If you feel that you can't go on, find someone whom you can trust and talk to them. I had my family and most of all, I had God and his word to lean on. In the process of becoming Debra Wright I learned how to find the courage to remain true to myself. When I let go of the limitations that others had placed on me, only then was I able to stand confidently in my own skin.

My question to you is, who are *you* becoming? God loves you and will never abandon you.

Just remember *"Weeping may endure for the night but joy comes in the morning."* Psalm 30:5.

This is a promise that you can always rely on. I have learned to love who I have become. So can you.

Your friend,<br>
Debra Wright

# GUIDED QUESTIONS

1. Throughout this book, we identified some issues that were prevalent in this marriage. How would you have handled this situation?
2. Losing a child at any stage is hard. Have you or anyone around you suffered this type of loss and what did you do?
3. Debra's faith in God allowed gave her the strength she needed, during her pregnancy. How would you cope if these challenges confronted you?
4. In Chapter 6, Debra spoke about a connection to an old flame, that she could not let go of. This created a chain of events that ultimately led her down a difficult and painful path. Soul ties are real, Have you had to deal with a past love and how did you handle it?

GUIDED QUESTIONS

5. Debra Walked away from her children and family during her divorce would you have left or stayed?
6. One of the central themes in this book is broken relationships and finding restoration. Have you had a broken relationship, Separation or divorce? What was your coping mechanism? How did you begin to heal?

**Debra Wright** is a native of Trinidad and Tobago and now resides in Ontario, Canada. She is a wife and mother of six children and grandmother to Her Grandson Roman.

Debra has been an event planner for over ten years and owns her own company Bloomingdale Wedding Couture and Events. She is also a speaker with a passion for helping women. Debra like to spend time with her husband and their family.

www.ingramcontent.com/pod-product-compliance
Lightning Source LLC
Chambersburg PA
CBHW071641080526
44586CB00013BA/1214